Food Webs

Ocean Food Chains

Emma Lynch

Heinemann Library
Chicago, Illinois

Photo research by Ruth Blair and Ginny Stroud-Lewis
Designed by Jo Hinton-Malivoire and AMR
Printed and bound in China by CTPS

10 09
10 9 8 7 6 5 4 3 2
ISBN 13: 9781403458643 (PB)

Library of Congress Cataloging-in-Publication Data
Lynch, Emma.
   Ocean food chains / Emma lynch.
      v. cm. — (Food webs)
   Includes bibliographical references (p.   ).
   Contents: What is an ocean food web? — What is an ocean food chain? — What is a producer in an ocean? — What is a primary consumer in an ocean? — What is a secondary consumer in an ocean? — What is a decomposer in an ocean? — How are ocean food chains different in different places? — What happens to a food web when a food chain breaks down? — How can we protect the environment and food chains?
   ISBN 1-4034-5857-X (lib. bdg.-hardcover) — ISBN 1-4034-5864-2 (pbk.)
  1. Marine ecology—Juvenile literature. 2. Food chains (Ecology)—Juvenile literature. [1. Marine ecology. 2. Food chains (Ecology) 3. Ecology.] I. Title. II. Series.
   QH541.5.S3L96 2004
   577.7—dc22

                                      2003026196

Acknowledgments
The author and publisher are grateful to the following for permission to reproduce copyright material:
Alamy p. **27** (Mr Vivak Gour-Broome); Corbis pp. **14** (Peter Johnson), **19** (Galen Rowell), **23** (Jeffrey L. Rotman), **24** (Martin Harvey/Gallo Images), pp. **8, 18**; Getty Images/Photodisc p. **25**; Harcourt Index/Digital Vision p. **5**; Heather Angel/Natural Visions pp. **7** (Norman T. Nicoll), p. **16**; Nature Picture Library pp. **12** (Jurgen Freund), **26** (Vincent Munier); NHPA pp. **11** (Pete Atkinson), **13** (Michael Patrick O'Neill), **22** (Daniel Heuclin); PA Photos p. **10**; SPL pp. **15** (Fred Winner/Jacana), **17** (Peter Scoones).

Cover photograph of a whale shark eating reproduced with permission of Bruce Coleman/Franco Banfi.

Illustrations by Words and Publications.

The publisher would like to thank Dr Dennis Radabaugh of the Department of Zoology at Ohio Wesleyan University for his comments in the preparation of this book.

Every effort has been made to contact copyright holders of any material reproduced in this book. Any omissions will be rectified in subsequent printings if notice is given to the publisher.

Contents

Some words are shown in bold, **like this**. You can find out
what they mean by looking in the glossary.

What Is an Ocean Food Web?

All living things are **organisms**. Organisms are eaten by other organisms. Small animals get eaten by bigger animals, who get eaten by even larger animals. When large animals die, they get eaten by tiny insects, maggots, and **bacteria**. Even mighty killer whales die and rot—then they are eaten by bacteria and **bottom feeders**. If you draw lines between the animals, showing who eats whom, you create a diagram called a food web.

The organisms in ocean **habitats** are part of a food web. In food web diagrams, the arrows lead from the food to the animal that eats it.

This food web is from the Atlantic Ocean.

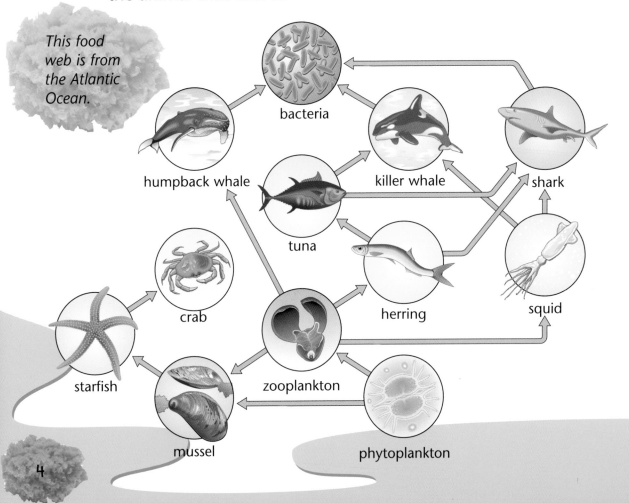

bacteria

humpback whale

killer whale

shark

tuna

herring

squid

crab

starfish

zooplankton

mussel

phytoplankton

4

What are ocean habitats like?

The oceans provide us with food, **minerals**, and **energy**. They are also important in controlling Earth's **climate**. Oceans are full of life. Certain plants and animals live in ocean habitats because they are especially suited to life there. They are part of the ocean food web because the plants or animals they feed on live in the ocean, too.

There are two main ocean habitats for animals: out in the open water, or on the ocean floor. Most kinds of fish and sea **mammals** live in open waters, or in **coral reefs** or rocky areas in the waters near the coast. Many other animals, such as crabs, snails, and sea worms, live on the ocean floor. Some live in holes they dig in the mud or sand of the seabed. Most **species** live in the first 350 feet (about 110 meters) of the ocean, where sunlight can still reach into the water. In deeper water, it becomes darker and colder, and there is less life.

Coral reefs in the warm shallow waters of tropical oceans are home to thousands of animals.

What is an ocean food chain?

A food web is made up of lots of different food chains. Food chains are simpler diagrams than food webs. They show the way some of the animals in a food web feed on each other. The arrows in the chain show the movement of food and **energy** from plants to animals as they feed on each other.

Most **organisms** are part of more than one food chain because they eat more than one type of food. This is safer for them. An organism that eats only one type of food will not survive if that food runs out.

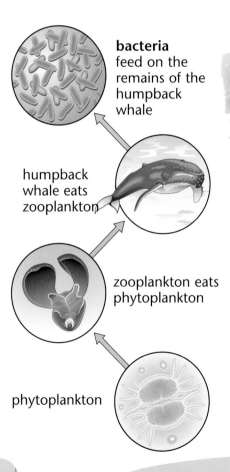

bacteria feed on the remains of the humpback whale

humpback whale eats zooplankton

zooplankton eats phytoplankton

phytoplankton

This diagram of an ocean food chain shows how energy passes from one link in the chain to another.

Starting the chain

Most food chains start with energy from the Sun. Plants such as **algae** trap the energy in sunlight and use it to make their own food. Seaweeds are large algae that look very much like plants on land. They have green, red, or brown fronds like leaves and hold tightly to rocks or to the seabed with their strong roots. Seaweeds grow well in shallow waters along shorelines, but not in deeper waters where there is almost no sunlight. There may seem to be no plant life at all in these deeper waters, but it is there.

Most plant life in the ocean is made up of **microscopic** plantlike organisms called phytoplankton. These drift around in the water near the sunny surface, taking energy from the Sun and growing in huge numbers. Many other animals in the sea eat phytoplankton and gain energy from them. These animals in turn are eaten by other animals. In this way, energy flows through the food chain and through the **habitat**.

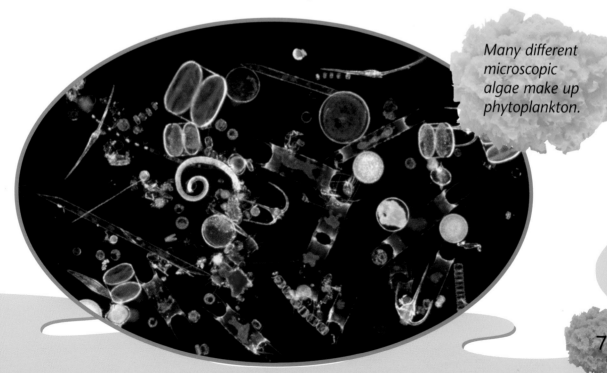

Many different microscopic algae make up phytoplankton.

Without sunlight, all the seaweeds and phytoplankton would die out. Phytoplankton make, or produce, more oxygen than all the plants on land. Without them, nearly all the **organisms** on our planet would die out.

Making the chain

Plants are called **producers**, because they trap the Sun's energy and produce food. Food chains usually start with producers. Animals are **consumers**, who have to eat other organisms to get **energy**. **Herbivores** are animals that eat plants. They are the **primary consumers** in a food chain. They often end up as food for meat-eating animals, known as **carnivores**. In food chains, we call these **secondary consumers**. Secondary consumers may also eat other secondary consumers, or feed on the remains of their **prey**. **Omnivores** eat plants as well as other animals. They are primary and secondary consumers.

Giant kelp is the largest type of seaweed. It grows in great "forests" in some coastal areas. The biggest kelps can reach nearly 100 feet (30 meters) tall.

More links in the chain

Food chains do not end with secondary consumers. All organisms eventually die. When this happens, their bodies are eaten by **scavengers** such as sea worms and **decomposers** such as **bacteria**. The waste from the decomposers sinks into the seabed and forms **nutrients**. When a current stirs up the seabed, the nutrients are swirled up toward the surface, where they can be taken in by the phytoplankton. In this way, the chain begins again.

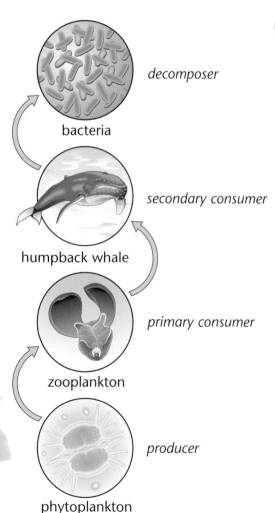

decomposer

bacteria

secondary consumer

humpback whale

primary consumer

zooplankton

producer

phytoplankton

This ocean food chain shows how energy moves from producer to primary consumer and then to secondary consumer and decomposer.

Breaking the chain

If some **organisms** in a food web die out, it may be deadly for the others. **Environmental** change, such as changes in **climate** or sea temperature, can affect **habitats**.

Human activity can cause breaks in ocean food chains and in natural cycles, too. **Pollution** from shipping and business poisons the water, and catching too many animals like anchovies, tuna, and whales puts these groups in danger. Oceans and seas are often connected, so disturbing the food chain of one habitat can affect other ocean life thousands of miles away.

Japanese whalers catch a minke whale in the Antarctic Ocean. Whaling for trade was banned in 1986 because too many were caught, but Japan still catches whales for what it calls "scientific purposes."

Which Producers Live in Oceans?

Plantlike **producers** called phytoplankton start ocean food chains. There are many **species** of phytoplankton, each with its own shape. Some are soft-bodied and can change shape.

Like plants on land, phytoplankton need sunlight, water, and **nutrients** to grow. Phytoplankton stay mostly near the surface to catch the sunlight. Currents push nutrients up from the seabed to the surface, where they are taken in by the phytoplankton. Phytoplankton are a main source of food for many other **microscopic** animals and small fish. In summer, they can grow in such huge numbers that the sea starts to look like a reddish brown soup. This is called a phytoplankton "bloom" or a "red tide."

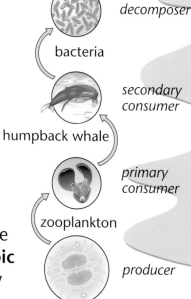

decomposer

bacteria

secondary consumer

humpback whale

primary consumer

zooplankton

producer

phytoplankton

"Red tides" like this are made up of billions of phytoplankton.

Seaweeds and other green plants like sea grasses and **algae** can be found nearer the shore in shallow waters. These plants are also important foods for small animals like sea urchins and big animals like dugongs and turtles.

Dugongs live mainly in shallow, tropical seas in western Australia. Just like Florida's manatees, they feed mostly on sea grasses and can grow to about 10 feet (3 meters) long.

Breaking the Chain: Producers

Phytoplankton are necessary to ocean food chains, but need certain conditions to grow. Currents of cold water containing **nutrients** rise up from the seabed, helping phytoplankton to grow. Some weather conditions make surface water warm. Warm water has already given up its nutrients, so there is no more food for the phytoplankton. As the phytoplankton starve, so do the fish and **mammals** that eat them.

Which Primary Consumers Live in Oceans?

Primary consumers are plant-eating animals. Phytoplankton are the most important source of plant food in the ocean. They are mostly eaten by the slightly larger zooplankton. Zooplankton is the name of a huge variety of tiny animals—some **microscopic**, others just a few inches long. They are all too small to swim against the ocean currents, and just drift where the water takes them. Zooplankton usually include the young of larger animals such as fish, squid, **mollusks**, and **crustaceans**. Some animals, called filter feeders, eat zooplankton by straining them from the water with their mouths. Zooplankton are also eaten by small fish, shrimp, and even whales!

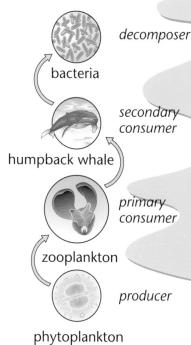

decomposer
bacteria

secondary consumer
humpback whale

primary consumer
zooplankton

producer
phytoplankton

*Sea slugs are mollusks that graze on seaweeds. They are often brightly colored. The colors warn **predators** that they have stinging cells on their backs.*

*Krill feed by filtering **algae** out of the water or scraping them off of the sea ice. They in turn are food for a whole range of other animals.*

Krill

Among the most important zooplankton animals are krill. Krill are small, shrimplike **crustaceans** found mostly in the Antarctic Ocean. They eat phytoplankton and are only about 0.5 to 2.5 inches (1–6 centimeters) long. Krill spend the day in deep waters, safe from most **predators**. At night, they swim up to the surface waters to feed on phytoplankton.

A single krill can lay up to 10,000 eggs, several times a year. If they have plenty of phytoplankton to eat, krill will also increase in numbers, turning the waters pink for many miles. The weight of krill in the Antarctic Ocean is estimated to reach 640 million tons (about 650 million tonnes) in the summer! Krill are among the most plentiful animals on Earth. They are a main source of food for many fish, squid, and seabirds. Their largest predators are **baleen** whales.

Which Secondary Consumers Live in Oceans?

Nearly all sea animals die when they are eaten by a **secondary consumer**. Some secondary consumers are small, like the barnacle that waves its featherlike feet in the water to catch zooplankton. They can also be enormous, like the blue whale that uses the hard **baleen** plates in its mouth to catch and eat krill.

Ocean predators

On the sea floor, there are many animals that are specially designed to attack their chosen **prey**. Starfish wrap themselves around **mollusks** such as oysters, and pull the shell apart to eat the animal inside.

In open waters, the huge manta ray simply opens its huge mouth and filters zooplankton and tiny fish from the water. The huge black marlin, one of the fastest fish in the sea, swims quickly through the surface waters chasing fast prey such as tuna, mackerel, and squid.

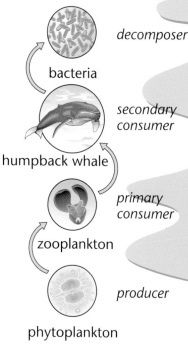

decomposer

bacteria

secondary consumer

humpback whale

primary consumer

zooplankton

producer

phytoplankton

A starfish puts its stomach inside a clam's shell and eats the clam while it is still in its shell.

15

Deep-sea predators

Deep in the ocean depths, **secondary consumers** have developed special ways of catching their **prey**. Many of the fish, squid, and shrimp here have organs on their skin that can produce light. They use these lights to attract prey or to dazzle a **predator**. Female anglerfish use their light organs to attract smaller fish and squid.

The largest of all deep-sea predators is the sperm whale. These hunt squid, large fish, and even deepwater sharks. Their favorite prey is the mysterious giant squid, an animal that has been found dead on beaches but has never been seen alive.

The light organ on the nose of this deep-sea anglerfish attracts prey. Its huge mouth can open to swallow prey bigger than itself.

Which Decomposers Live in Oceans?

Decomposers are the other major group in a food web. They feed on the remains of dead animals and plants, and their waste. **Bacteria** are ocean decomposers. They break down dead animals and plants into simpler substances, such as **nutrients**. Phytoplankton take in the nutrients that are made in this process, and so the food chain starts all over again.

Animals that help decomposers

When animals die, other animals known as **scavengers** eat them and break them down into smaller bits that decomposers can use. Scavengers may be **bottom feeders** like crabs and lobsters, or may be small fish and even sharks.

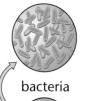
decomposer

bacteria

secondary consumer

humpback whale

primary consumer

zooplankton

producer

phytoplankton

Many scavengers will feed on this dead whale's body, or carcass. Some smaller scavengers, such as crabs and sea worms, may live on its remains for up to 50 years!

Sea cucumbers are strange tubelike **scavengers** that move slowly along the seabed. They shovel sand into their mouths with their feelers and suck out any decaying animal and plant matter from the sand.

Sea urchins feed by scooping **algae** into their mouths with the shovellike teeth under their bodies. They are covered in very sharp spines to protect them from **predators**. Sea urchins live on the ocean floor, and can move slowly on soft tubelike feet.

*Some sea cucumbers are brightly colored and seem to be easy **prey** for fish, but they are often poisonous.*

How Are Ocean Food Chains Different in Different Places?

Although oceans share many features, their food chains can be very different. They are affected by the **climate**, the currents and depth of the water, and by the life living nearby. Human activity will also affect them.

The Antarctic Ocean

The Antarctic Ocean is the fourth largest ocean in the world. It surrounds the continent of Antarctica. Severe storms, strong winds, huge icebergs, and sea ice are found here. The animals that live here are specially designed for life in a harsh climate.

Many **species** of seals live here, including the fur seal and elephant seal. Too many seals were once hunted for their oil and skin, but they are now protected. Although seals spend a lot of time on land, they hunt in the sea for fish and krill.

Elephant seals like these are found throughout the Antarctic Ocean. They feed mainly on squid and fish.

One large **predator** in the Antarctic Ocean is the leopard seal. It has spotted fur, like a leopard, and is a fierce hunter. It eats krill, but also hunts penguins, squid, fish, and other seals. It can even jump out of the water to snatch penguins off of the ice.

Several **species** of penguins live in the water and ice of the Antarctic Ocean. Chinstrap, macaroni, and king penguins are all here, feeding on huge numbers of fish and krill.

Krill is the main source of food for many animals in the Antarctic Ocean. Some of the world's most **endangered** whales, such as the blue, finback, sei, and humpback whales, come here in the summer to eat tons of krill.

This is a food chain from the Antarctic Ocean.

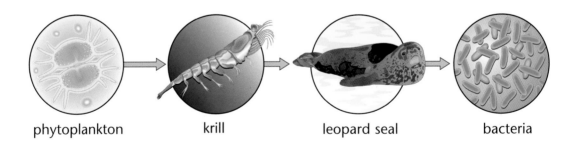

| phytoplankton | krill | leopard seal | bacteria |

The Pacific Ocean

The Great Barrier Reef is found in the Pacific Ocean, off the northeast coast of Australia. It contains the world's largest collection of **coral reefs**. Coral reefs are ideal **habitats** for many rare species. Small animals like sea snails move slowly over the coral, feeding on **algae**. The coral itself is nibbled by smaller fish or bitten off in big chunks by parrot-jawed triggerfish. Sea grasses provide food for green turtles and dugongs. Once the sea grasses die, they begin to rot and are eaten by sea cucumbers, crabs, and sea worms.

Large predators roam the reefs looking for **prey**. Barracuda can grow up to 6 feet (2 meters) long and often hunt in packs. They open their mouths wide to bite other large fish, chopping them in half. The green turtle's only predator is the tiger shark. The tiger shark will eat almost anything, including trash!

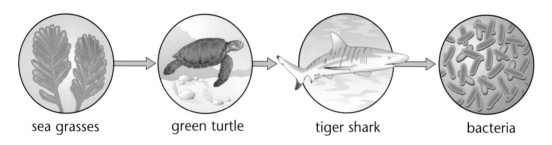

sea grasses   green turtle   tiger shark   bacteria

This is a food chain from the Great Barrier Reef. It includes the green turtle, one of six species of marine turtles that can be found in the Great Barrier Reef.

What Happens to a Food Web When a Food Chain Breaks Down?

All around the world, ocean food chains and webs are at risk because of humans. Although much work is under way to stop more harm from being done, these are some of the dangers currently faced by plants and animals in ocean **habitats**.

Pollution

One of the biggest dangers to ocean food webs is from **pollution**. We pollute the oceans with waste from our homes, farms, and factories. Pollution in the sea can also harm human life. Tiny plankton take in the poisons we put in seawater. When they are eaten by small fish and shellfish, the poison passes along the food chain, until at some point an animal that has taken in these poisons is caught and eaten by humans.

*Trash thrown into the sea or onto beaches harms the **environment** and the animals within it.*

Industry

Oil and gravel occur naturally in oceans. When we take them from the seabed, we often disturb the places where new fish are born—and this reduces fish numbers. At the same time, we may pollute the oceans, especially with oil. It can cover the water for many miles and can wash onto coastal rocks, where it kills beds of mussels and pollutes rock pools and beaches. Droplets of oil sink beneath the surface, where they poison sea life.

Overfishing

Too much fishing of any **species** can upset the food chain. Over the last century, humans have overfished many species, and numbers of herring, cod, and anchovies have been drastically reduced. Although there are now some agreements in place to limit fishing, it is hard to make sure they are being obeyed. Except for areas near the coast, the ocean does not belong to any country, so governments cannot do much to protect ocean life.

Seabirds like this penguin can get covered in oil from an oil slick. They become too heavy to fly, or die from poisoning as they try to clean their feathers.

A bottle-nosed dolphin swims near a drift net. These long nets are meant to catch tuna, but animals such as dolphins and sharks also get trapped in them and die.

Breaking the Chain: How We Are Affected

When animals and plants are poisoned, killed, or driven out of their **habitats**, it creates breaks in food chains and affects the entire food web of that area. Eventually, breaks or changes to food chains and webs affect us, too. For example, in the last century, thousands of people in and near Minamata, Japan, died or were injured as a result of mercury poisoning. They had eaten fish from water that had been polluted with mercury by a local company. The protection of ocean food webs is important for all living things.

How Can We Protect Ocean Food Chains?

All around the world, scientists, governments and other groups are working to clean up and protect oceans and ocean food chains. They want to make sure that no more harm is done to these **habitats** and the animals and plants that depend on them.

International research and protection

Scientists make surveys of ocean habitats. They test the water quality and **pollution** levels, and they check animal and plant life to make sure that their population levels are not falling. In this way, scientists find the links in the food web that need protection.

Scientists tell governments how they can improve and protect ocean habitats. Governments around the world work together to create agreements that will protect ocean life and prevent illegal fishing.

Much of this work has come too late for some **species**, but at least these agreements now give some protection to species that provide food for many other animals.

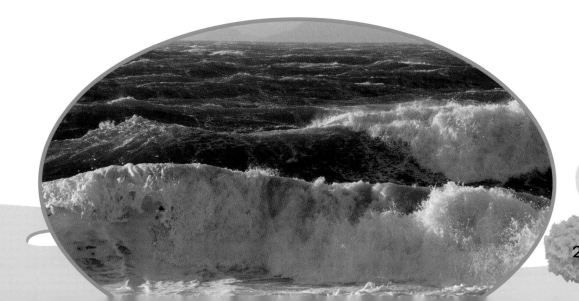

An oil spill from the tanker Erika polluted this beach in Brittany, France, in 1999. These volunteers are cleaning up and looking for seabirds covered in oil.

Ocean conservation

Groups like Friends of the Earth, Greenpeace, and the World Wildlife Fund work to make sure that governments take care of the oceans. Many countries are part of the International Convention for the Prevention of **Pollution** from Ships. This group works to protect coasts and seas from pollution from ships, oil, and waste.

Conservation groups try to show people living near oceans how they can help to protect them, for everyone's future. All around the world, cleanup operations are trying to limit the amount of damage caused by pollution. More than 130 countries are now part of the United Nations Environment Program, with plans to tackle pollution in some of the world's dirtiest oceans.

Research an ocean food web

Although it takes special equipment to do deep ocean research, you can study **habitats** near the ocean. If you go to the seaside, think about the food chains there. Look in the rock pools and along the water's edge. Here are some suggestions to help you find out about animal and plant life.

1. What is the habitat like? Is it cold or warm, shady or light?
2. Can you see any plants or animals? Put them in groups that are similar, such as plants, birds, fish, and **crustaceans**.
3. What do you think each animal would like to eat?
4. Which are the **predators** and which are the **prey**?
5. Can you make a food chain of the animals and plants you see?
6. Think about how the habitat could change. How would these changes affect the wildlife there?

This beach in Cornwall, England, is home to the hundreds of creatures that live in the rock pools and along the shoreline.

Where Are the World's Main Oceans?

This map shows the location of the main oceans of the world. The Pacific Ocean is the largest, followed by the Atlantic, Indian, and Antarctic Oceans. The Arctic Ocean is the smallest.

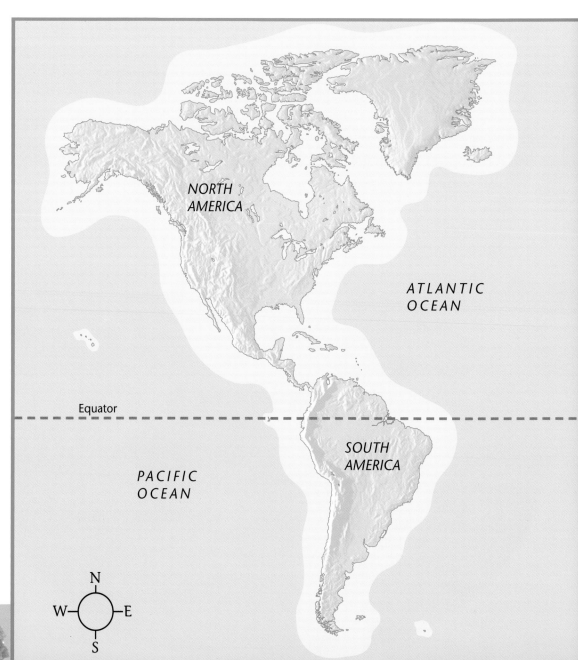

NORTH AMERICA

ATLANTIC OCEAN

Equator

SOUTH AMERICA

PACIFIC OCEAN

N
W — E
S

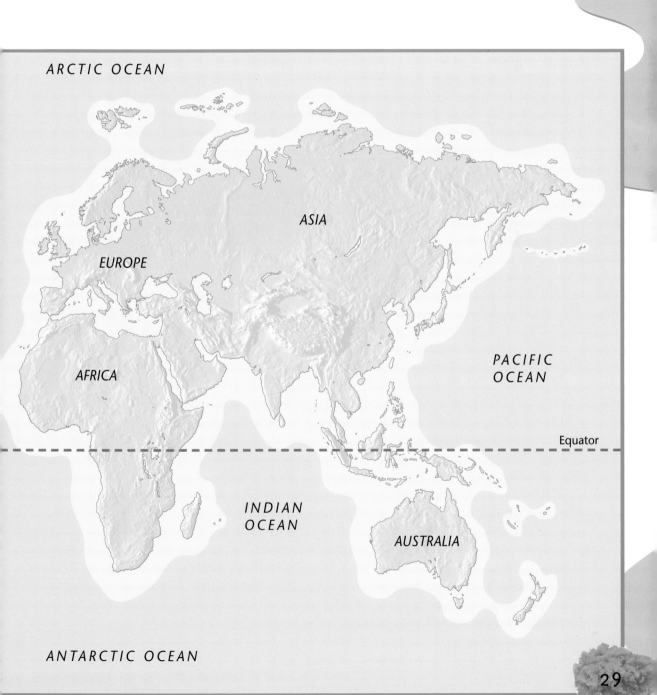

ARCTIC OCEAN

EUROPE

ASIA

AFRICA

PACIFIC
OCEAN

Equator

INDIAN
OCEAN

AUSTRALIA

ANTARCTIC OCEAN

29

Glossary

algae (singular alga) small plantlike organisms

bacteria (singular bacterium) tiny living decomposers found everywhere

baleen hard layers on the upper jaw of some whales, used to filter plankton from the water

bottom feeder animal that finds its food on the seabed

carnivore animal that eats the flesh of another animal

climate general conditions of weather in any area

conservation protecting and saving the natural environment

consumer organism that eats other organisms

coral reef ridge of rocks formed from the skeletons of many tiny jellylike animals called polyps

crustacean hard-shelled animal that mainly lives in water, such as a crab, lobster, or shrimp

decomposer organism that breaks down and gets nutrients from dead plants and animals and their waste

endangered at risk of dying out completely, as a species of plant or animal

energy power to grow, move, and do things

environment surroundings in which an animal or plant lives, including the other animals and plants that live there

habitat place where an organism lives

herbivore animal that eats plants

mammal animal that feeds its babies on milk from its own body

microscopic too small to be seen without a microscope

mineral substance that occurs naturally and is not made from plant or animal matter, such as a rock or metal

mollusk soft-bodied animal, often with a hard shell, such as a snail, oyster, or octopus

nutrient chemical that plants and animals need to live

omnivore animal that eats both plants and other animals

organism living thing

pollution when chemicals or other substances that can damage animal or plant life escape into water, soil, or the air

predator animal that hunts and eats other animals

prey animal that is caught and eaten by a predator

primary consumer animal that eats plants

producer organism (plant) that can make its own food

scavenger organism that feeds on dead plant and animal material and waste

secondary consumer animal that eats primary consumers and other secondary consumers

species group of organisms that are similar to each other and can breed together to produce young

More Books to Read

Dalgleish, Sharon. *Ocean Life*. Broomall, PA: Mason Crest, 2002.

Donovan, Sandy. *Ocean Animals*. Chicago, IL: Raintree, 2003.

Goodman, Susan. *Ultimate Field Trip 3: Wading into Marine Biology*. New York: Simon and Schuster, 2000.

Lauber, Patricia. *Who Eats What?* New York: HarperCollins, 2001.

Littlefield, Cindy. *Awesome Ocean Science: Investigating the Secrets of the Underwater World*. Charlotte, Vt.: Williamson Publishing, 2002.

Llewellyn, Claire. *Animal Atlas*. Santa Monica, CA: Creative Publishing, 2003.

Meucci, Antonella. *Seas and Oceans*. Milwaukee: Gareth Stevens, 2000.

Morey, Allan. *Ocean Food Chains*. Minneapolis, MN: Lake Street Publishers, 2003.

Steele, Christy. *Oceans*. Chicago: Raintree, 2001.

Williams, Andy. *Nature Unfolds the Oceans*. New York: Crabtree Publishing, 2002.

Index